my first Gardening ABC Picture Book

This book belongs to:

_____

My First Gardening ABC Picture Book © 2022 MadGaviette Publishing
All rights reserved. No part of this book may be used or reproduced in any manner whatsoever without written permissions.

A is for Apron

B is for Bulbs

C is for Compost

D is for Dirt

E is for Evergreen

F is for Flowerbed

G is for Gloves

H is for
Hoe

I is for Irrigation

J is for Jardiniere

K is for Kids

L is for
Leaf

M is for
Manure

N is for Natural Sunlight

O is for Organic Food

P is for Pitchfork

Q is for Quality Tools

R is for Roots

S is for Seeds

T is for Trowel

U is for Underground

V is for Vegetables

FRESH VEGETABLES

W is for Wheelbarrow

X is for Xeriscape

Y is for
Yard

Z is for Zones

Happy Gardening!